For Rosalie, Hayley and Claire

And for Edward who, wherever he is, will

always be with me

Introduction

Edward Mellish was a completely ordinary man. He was good-looking without being movie-star handsome. He was bright but not an Einstein or Hawking. He lived as most of us do – he worked, first in jobs he didn't much care for, and later doing things he loved for an organization whose mission inspired him. He had day-to-day ups and down the way all of us do. There was nothing specifically unique about Edward.

Yet Edward was the most extraordinary person I have ever known. The things in Edward that combined to make him the person he was made him, somehow, completely unlike anyone else.

While I have never been able to capture or quantify just what made this true, I was aware of it every day during the 10 years that I was able to call him my friend. I was blessed to have been his friend, and I am blessed to have the memory of our friendship and everything that came to me because of it.

Whatever and whoever I am today, I would not be the same had I not met Edward. Our friendship did a lot to heal parts of me I had thought were irretrievably broken.

I could never have thanked him enough. I will never forget him.

When someone is frail, most people's instinct is to step back. Real friends come closer. You have been the best of the best.

The words were spoken by my friend Edward in a whisper. I had to lean over the railing of his rented hospital bed to hear them. We were in the living room of a third floor condo, it was a stiflingly hot August day in Chicago, and there was no air conditioning. I didn't notice.

I stood silently, scared and helpless in the face of the inevitably of what was coming. I didn't know what to say.

When I saw him the next day he could not speak. The day after he was in a coma.

And then he died.

Potassium Stick

Edward told me once that we became friends because of a banana. I had taken a secretarial job at Planned Parenthood, where he and Rosalie were both working, and I met Edward on my first day there in April of 1984. I met lots of people that day, but Edward stood out because I had seen him already, before we were introduced. He had been furiously kicking the copy machine.

Anyway, sometime during those first days of a new job, trying to get used to working again after three of unemployment, I was walking back to my office eating a banana. Edward and I passed each other in the hall and I held up the banana as I walked and said "Potassium stick." I can't say that it occurred to me that we became friends at that minute, but I do remember that he laughed in a surprised way.

I was a mess by the time I started working at Planned Parenthood. I had worked full time for 7 years before that, having left college after one semester. After a year as an answering service operator (I was the youngest employee there by about 45 years), I spent three years at a large company working my way UP to a secretarial position, which was a challenge considering that I did not type or take shorthand, and I hated filing. Walking away toward what I hoped would be bigger and better things, I went on to a supervisor position at CASS Communications, a place that will always, no matter what I do for the rest of my life, be the worst job I ever had. Hating every minute of every day for the three years I was there, I refused to admit I had made a bad choice, so I stayed, feeling worse about the place, everyone in it and myself every day, until finally my co-workers went to our boss en masse and said it was me or them. They let me go. I wasn't sorry, but I was royally pissed.

During my period of unemployment, I spent every day reminding myself that I had no discernible skills or education and was not equipped to do anything. A friend of mine worked at Planned Parenthood and told me about an opening there, in the Development Department. At the time, I didn't know what Development was. It turned out to be fundraising.

The available position was the Development secretary, but I had long-since resigned myself that I'd be lucky to go back to secretarial work. I applied for and was offered the job – the salary was 20% lower than what I had been earning, but I kind of felt like I deserved that. And, as was typical for me, I thought if I got there and worked really hard, my efforts would be recognized in ways I found acceptable.

Somehow, starting that job felt like coming home. I felt really comfortable there. Part of it, I suppose, was a sense of my own inadequacies, and my feeling that I deserved to be punished in some way for having tried to be better than I was. It was almost a relief to be back doing work I had wanted to move away from. And the people there were much more diverse and interesting than those I had just left.

There was Barbara, my office mate, who went out of her way to be friendly and make me feel welcome; Doris, my boss, who at 65 was the most dynamic person I'd ever worked for; Nancy, the friend who told me about the job opening, who was a typical friend of mine – kind of messed up, struggling with alcohol problems, relationship problems, etc. And then there was this tall, dark-haired guy who greeted me with a friendly smile when we were introduced, not realizing I'd just seen him swearing at and kicking the copy machine...

I think Edward's ongoing battles with the copy machine were the only signs of anger or negative emotion I saw from him until well after his diagnosis. For someone so consistently affable, it amazed me to see him pounding on the thing and kicking it. I didn't get how someone whose job it was to make dozens of copies every week could hate the machine so much.

Eventually I learned that he had taken a job as assistant to the Executive Director thinking that it would enable him to work his way up to Executive Director. As soon as I knew that, his frustration made perfect sense, although I still don't know on what he based the idea that he was following a logical career path.

When I found out that Edward had the ED job as a goal, I almost labeled him "loser" like so many of the men who gravitated to me. I'd had my fair share by then – I had been tossed aside by (in chronological order) David, nine years my senior, who lost patience with my desire not to relinquish my virginity at 16.... Kirk, who decided to date someone else six weeks after we met and I instantly fell in love with him..... (The first "someone else" was a girl, but shortly after we finished high school, Kirk came out as a homosexual.) Michael, the man to whom I did relinquish my virginity at age 20, who was clinically depressed and made a half-hearted attempt at suicide, after which I received a phone call from his mother, who asked to see me in order to tell me in person that she didn't want her son dating a Jewish girl.... Dave, an alcoholic who worked at CASS with me, who used to literally steal money from his daughter's piggy bank to buy himself beer....

I ostensibly gave up on men at 23, although I continued to view every man I met as a possible partner. I was so – I don't know, maybe jaded is the right word, maybe wounded – that I looked for reasons to avoid every man I met even as I wondered if he'd "like me."

When I met Edward, I thought he was gay. He reminded me of Kirk in some ways, and I thought perhaps it would be best to steer clear of Edward. Believe me, when you learn that a guy is so not into you that he gives up on your gender, you go to great lengths to avoid ever going through anything like that again.

My suspicions gave me a safe distance, I thought. Nothing was more important to me at that time than making sure I didn't get hurt any more. I just couldn't handle it.

But man, I couldn't resist that laugh. It made me feel appreciated and valued. I didn't do anything to try to impress him, I didn't give him anything or try to be someone else, I just walked by and said something. And he laughed, and suddenly, I wanted to be his friend. I wanted to hear that laugh again.

Soon after, I learned from being in an elevator with Edward and a woman I had not been introduced to that Edward was not gay – he was living with and preparing to marry Rosalie, who I eventually learned worked in the clinic at Planned Parenthood.

Edward actually invited me to the wedding a few days after we met. At that time, I had never spoken to Rosalie and barely knew Edward, and I thought he was issuing the invitation to make me feel at home at Planned Parenthood. So I declined the invitation.

In retrospect, I think that I was wrong. I think Edward really wanted me to be there. And I don't think he would have asked me if he hadn't hoped I'd attend.

In any event, as I had already mentally crossed Edward off my list of potential loves of my life, I relaxed and we settled into an enjoyable work friendship.

It was very, very pale.

A few weeks after we met, Edward invited me to come to his apartment, along with several other people, to help get out a mailing for something called Personal Pac. I had some vague knowledge that this was a political thing, but in those days I had no interest in politics and even less interest in sitting around stuffing envelopes on a Saturday afternoon with a bunch of people I didn't know.

However, in the interest of making new friends in my new job, and in the face of the reality that I had nothing better to do, I said I'd go. Personal Pac turned out to be a political action committee started by one of the women on the Planned Parenthood Board of Directors – a dragon lady named Marcie who, as a pro-choice Republican, tried to get the "right" people elected to public office.

The work was as dull as I expected it to be – stapling and stuffing. But it was a pretty fun afternoon anyway. It was the first time I spoke with Rosalie. I don't think we were formally introduced until that day. I had only seen her a couple of times at the office, once in the elevator with Edward, where as I recall she sounded annoyed that he had left without her that morning; and again in an all-staff meeting, when she had raised a few questions relating to the clinic that caused someone else in the room to raise their hand and ask, "Excuse me – who are you?"

All I had gotten from my encounters with Rosalie till that day were the knowledge that Edward was not, as I had initially suspected, gay, and the feeling that Rosalie was not exactly the nicest person I had ever come across.

I remember very little of the conversation at their home that Saturday. I only remember that I got bored sitting and stapling papers together with a small stapler that worked only every so often, and I went into the kitchen where Rosalie was preparing some snack type thing.

As we chatted I was surprised by how similar we seemed to be. I got a taste that day of her sense of humor (very like mine), the kindness and generosity in her nature, and some of her opinions (in line with mine). It was like opening a box to find a gift you'd been wanting for years and didn't even know you needed till it was in front of you.

I went there to help out because I liked Edward very much from the minute I met him, and I wanted us to be friends. But I remember two things about the afternoon. One was my discovery of who Rosalie really is.

The other came while she and I were talking in the kitchen and Edward was in the back of the apartment. The phone rang, a funny, soft, almost inaudible ring. We heard it because there was a phone near where we were standing.

Rosalie took the call and was just finishing the conversation when Edward came back. She hung up the phone and told him who had called. He said he had not heard the phone ring, and I lowered my voice to a near-whisper and said, "It was very, very pale."

And he looked at me with sheer delight in his eyes and his smile – the first of many of those smiles he blessed me with during the years we were friends. I've never known anyone else who was so unafraid to show his appreciation for others so easily and so enthusiastically.

I carry that smile with me even now. And I think about how all of us sometimes feel unappreciated and under-valued in our day-to-day life, and what a gift that smile was in reminding me that the opposite is also true.

I remember a lot of Edward's smiles – there was a big "happy to see you" grin, a wry, crooked, "how could I have done that" sort of thing, and one, with a lot of eyes involved, that was reserved for the people he loved the most.

That day turned out to be a typical one in our relationship, the three of us – it started out with me thinking I was giving something to them, but I ended up getting much more in return.

God be with you, Cheryl

I've had my doubts about God over the years. I am a Jewish woman, raised without very much attention paid to God or religion. I did go to religious school for several years (Sabbath School – on Saturdays) and when I turned 8, I was asked if I wanted to go to Hebrew School and prepare to be Bat Mitvzahed at 13. I asked my brother, Howard, who is a year older than me and already had a year under his belt, if he thought I should go. He said no, it was horrible, it was hard to learn and took too much time and I'd be crazy to do it if I didn't have to. (He, being the first-born and a boy, was not given a choice.) So I didn't go, and regretted the decision only once, 4 years later when Howard spent 15 minutes reading Hebrew in temple and then went to a party in his honor where people handed him checks all afternoon. His speech to the guests at his party began with the words "I'd like to thank you all for my bulging pockets."

God and Judaism were one to me, and I don't remember any emphasis being placed on either in my childhood. My religious training ended when Howard's did, and I was not mandated to attend services after that. As I moved through my teenage years, my family changed dramatically, with my parents separating several times before finally divorcing when I was 18.

I began to question God's existence at 15 or 16, and made a conscious and verbal choice to reject Him. For much of the next 10 years I meandered through life without Him.

When I did come across Him, it was by invitations from friends, none of whom were Jewish. I attended a few weddings, a baptism here and there. I enjoyed the experiences – seeing how other religions did things, and being reminded that there were people who believed that God existed. But I experienced it all remotely – it never felt personal to me.

In the early years of our friendship, Edward and Rosalie went to midnight mass on Christmas Eve. When I moved to an apartment a block from theirs in 1988, I invited them to spend Christmas Eve with me, and they asked if I'd like to join them for midnight mass. I thought it might be fun – they described it to me as "the smells and bells service" -- so I agreed to go.

It was a cold night, and because the church is in a congested area of the city, we had to park a few blocks away and walk, which was quite an invigorating experience at midnight.

I remember that the inside of the church, which I had passed thousands of times over a lifetime lived in Chicago, was bigger than I expected it to be, and packed with people. The service included priests dressed very ornately and holding containers of lit incense attached to chains which they swung back and forth as they went up and down the aisles. It looked and smelled nothing like any church service I had ever seen.

I confess I didn't pay strict attention to the service – it was more of a spectacle to me than a religious experience. It ended, though, with the priest urging the congregation to stand, and for each person to turn to their neighbor and wish for them the presence of God in their lives. I had seen this sort of thing before in other churches, and always dreaded it, because always in a church I was an outsider, and I could never get used to having strangers wish me well for no reason or shake my hand.

This night, though, it was not a stranger who turned to me, but Edward, who suddenly had a different light in his eyes, and who said "God be with you, Cheryl" in a voice so warm and filled with good will and friendship that I can still hear the words in my head today. For the first time, those words had real meaning for me.

With five simple words, he started me on a path to find my own connection to God, my understanding that we share the same God, and my identity as a Jew; a path that led back to a sense of a part of myself without which I could never have felt complete.

Cook, Buddy

When I first became friendly with Edward and Rosalie, I was living in a small apartment about 5 miles away from their condo. I was working a lot and not doing much of anything else, including cleaning my apartment, so I never had anyone over, because I would have been embarrassed to let them in the door. I also never had enough money – secretarial work at a non-profit social service organization is about as far from financially rewarding as you can get, and the three months of unemployment before I started at Planned Parenthood really threw my finances into the proverbial toilet.

I left Planned Parenthood in 1987, and for the first time I took a job that paid me enough money to live on and had some promise of professional growth.

After struggling financially for 10 years, I could move to a larger apartment in a better neighborhood and hire a cleaning person to come in regularly.

The neighborhood I wanted to move to was the one in which Edward and Rosalie were living. After a Thanksgiving dinner with them on an uncommonly warm Chicago night in 1986, we had gone out to walk off our dinner. Barely a block from their apartment, there was what seemed magical to me -- a little park, tucked away in the middle of the city neighborhood. It had a kids' playground, a big duck pond, tennis courts, very cool castle-style apartment buildings fronting it, and best of all, a tiny zoo! I fell in love with Indian Boundary Park that night and from then on, I wanted to live near it.

When I was able to afford a move, I looked around for a few months without finding anything that I liked that I could really afford. Then one day I was shown a place a block away from Edward and Rosalie. It was really perfect for me, and I liked everything about it except that it was a block away from their condo building. I was beginning to value their friendship so much that I didn't want to do anything to jeopardize it, and I thought they might not like the idea of me being that close. In the end I called them to ask if they thought it would be a problem, and Edward gave me their blessing to become a neighbor.

I got settled in, found a cleaning person to keep my new place habitable, and settled into my new life. When I had lived at my mother's and was dating the clinically-depressed Michael, who was always short of cash, I learned to cook a few things so I could make dinners for him, rather than eating out every night. Now, 12 years later, I had a kitchen I could turn around in and friends nearby for whom I could cook. I invited Edward and Rosalie over for dinner once a month or so.

I bought cookbooks and tried something new every time. They'd sometimes bring dessert or wine. I loved those evenings. I loved having space I could share, and people I wanted to share it with. I loved sitting around after dinner, savoring the meal and the conversation.

At bottom, of course, I was still me on those evenings, meaning that I was sometimes not in a great mood. I was seeing a counselor regularly, working very hard at things with which I was not yet comfortable, so it was not unusual for me to be upset about some perceived work deficiency or failure, or some issue that came up in a counseling session. Most times, though, even if I wasn't feeling great when they arrived, I'd be much better within the first half hour.

One night, though, I was just in a horrible mood, and I couldn't shake it. I was near tears all through dinner.

I tried to apologize to them, but they seemed completely unaffected by my mood -- Rosalie said I could behave any way I wanted to in my own home.

Usually when they visited I turned on some music after dinner. In an attempt at normalcy, I started a Buddy Holly CD and when Edward heard the opening bars of *Peggy Sue*, he lowered his voice about 4 octaves and said to himself, "Cook, Buddy."

It cracked me up. I don't know what was struck me so funny about it, but all at once I was laughing and enjoying myself and happy to be alive. The amazing thing is that they were both fine either way. It didn't bother them that I had invited them over and couldn't even smile at them for the first hour or two that they were there. And they were equally unperturbed by my sudden turnaround – they just welcomed me into the evening and we all went on from there.

You hold him down and I'll hit him

I defy anyone to convince me that there are better friends than Edward and Rosalie. When I moved into my own apartment near Indian Boundary Park, the unit had really horrible, old, dingy carpeting in the living room, dining room and bedroom.

I made arrangements to have new carpeting installed before my furniture was moved in, and I didn't want to have to pay the carpet installers to remove the old carpet. Edward and Rosalie offered to help pull up the old carpet, so we scheduled a "party" for the work to get done.

I should say right here that I'm not particularly handy around the house. While I don't exactly fully embrace the "Jewish princess" role which is occasionally ascribed to me, it's true that I'm never really excited about the prospect of performing manual labor.

Also, once the work began, it turned out that the padding under the old horrible carpet was actually old, horrible horsehair or something that shredded when it was touched, and it had been glued to the floor. This meant that removing it involved several hours of a scraping sound that was remarkably like nails on a chalkboard. I thought I was going to lose my mind.

Not only did I not help in the work being done on my own floors, I could barely stand to remain in the apartment, let alone a room in which the work was being done. So it ended up that Edward and Rosalie, along with, I believe, a few other friends, did all of the work while I tried to remain in the space without shrieking.

A couple of years later, Edward and Rosalie did some renovations in their kitchen which included the installation of black and white floor tiles. I loved the way their floor looked, and my kitchen had 40-year-old tiles that were starting to peel away a bit, so I got some black and white tiles for my kitchen.

This time it was just the three of us. Edward and Rosalie came over with some tools (me being a princess, I was not very tool-rich) and Edward took control of the project, saying that we needed to pull up the old tiles before laying down the new.

We spent several hours struggling with the old tile, using some kind of heated thing to melt the glue to allow us to remove tiles. Some of the tiles split when we tried to pull them up, others cracked, others just wouldn't budge.

Finally we took a break. While we were regaining our strength for another go with the old tiles, Rosalie idly picked up a piece of paper from inside a box of the new tiles and began reading it. The paper was a sheet of installation instructions which began with the words, "Do not remove existing tile. You will have better results if you install on top of existing tile." She read this aloud, and we both looked at Edward, who had this wonderfully abashed look on his face. Then she looked at me and said "You hold him down, and I'll hit him."

I've been known to giggle. I started as soon as the words were out of her mouth, and soon we were all literally rolling on the floor laughing until tears were streaming down our faces.

The floor was ultimately finished and of course I had to leave it there a few years later when I moved – but the memory of its installation still makes me smile.

Do you want us to come over?

Growing up in a suburb of Chicago, my family had a dog. I love dogs and we were, somehow, a dog family overall, I think. When I was a senior in high school, my mother's sister Susan, who had 3 cats, married a man who was allergic to cat hair, and Susan convinced my mother to take 2 of the 3 cats. One of them, Abbie, adopted me. She was afraid of our dog, so she spent the entire day hiding under my bed and when I came home in the afternoon she'd jump onto it to greet me and she hung out with me in my room all the time. The dog, Farfel, was a German shepherd mix who liked my mother best because she fed him. I think it's easy to understand that I fell hard for the blind adoration from the cat.

When I went away to college (for what turned out to be only 3 months) my mother said we had to give Abbie away, because without me in the house she would be very unhappy. I gave her to a woman with a 3-year-old girl that I used to babysit for. I was excited about having her go to someone I knew because then I could still visit her. During my first visit home, I went to visit Abbie and she clearly had not the slightest idea who I was. So much for blind adoration. Cats love the ones they're with.

Soon after that, my erstwhile boyfriend-turned-homosexual Kirk found a stray cat and convinced my mother to let me take her. I named her Minerva, because she was a beautiful, completely black cat and I thought she deserved the name of a goddess. After our dog died I adopted another cat (Zachary, a grey and white studly-looking cat) from a friend and brought in a third one which was supposed to be a pet for the children of the man my mother was dating. The third cat, Timmy (a long-haired orange tabby), contracted a virus the day I brought him home, and by the time my mom and I (mostly my mom) nursed him through it we didn't want to part with him, so we ended up with 3 cats, all of whom I took with me when I left home the following year.

Cats are the best pets for lazy apartment-dwellers, especially in Chicago where you REALLY have to look hard to find a landlord that will let you have a dog, even if you want to walk one. My cats were good pets. Zachary and Timmy had arrived together and became friends, and Minerva was quite simply the best cat that ever lived. She always came when I called her and spent exactly the right amount of time with me. She never let me feel lonely for her but never overstayed her welcome. She purred contentedly a lot, slept my pillow, moved uncomplainingly if I tossed and turned at night -- the very picture of pet perfection.

Let me go on record here as saying I am not one of those people for whom pets are like children. I know that cats are animals and not people, okay? But I did enjoy the company, I enjoyed watching Zach and Timmy play together, and I loved them all.

I had Minerva for about 13 years, and suddenly one day in 1989 I realized that she was sick. Very, very sick. I knew before I took her to the vet that something was very wrong with her. Even the night before I took her in, she still came when I called her, struggling to find the energy to walk from the bedroom to the den and jump into my lap. I remember stroking her and whispering, asking her not to leave me, knowing the words were both ridiculous and futile, but unable to stop myself from saying them.

As soon as the vet examined her, he said she should be put to sleep. He told me he would operate if I wanted him to, but she was an old cat and he didn't feel recovery would be easy for her, and in any case he felt that she could not live long after the surgery. He felt the humane thing to do was to let her go. And so I did.

I left his office with the empty carrier feeling totally lost. In tears, I went to my mother's office, a few blocks away, and told her, and then I went home. I thought I had pulled myself together a bit, but walking in without Minerva it hit me all over again, and I went to the phone and called Rosalie and Edward.

The phone woke them up - it was about 9:00 on a Saturday morning, and I could hear how sleepy Rosalie sounded when she said hello. I sobbed out a "Hi," and she was instantly awake, asking what was wrong. I told her I had had to have Minerva put to sleep, and she just said "Do you want us to come over?"

And I said yes. Never in my life had I allowed myself to impose upon friends that way. What ineffable relief I felt when the doorbell rang, and two people came in and hugged me and I knew it was okay to be sad and to feel loss.

We talked about my cats (present and absent), about their cat Garland, who had been Edward's cat before he and Rosalie met. I remember him saying he knew he would have to face losing Garland one day, and how he dreaded it.

I don't remember how long they stayed, or anything much about that day or the ones following. But I will always remember that sleepy voice offering love and comfort.

Oh – you mean the dish?

Edward loved Rosalie with everything he had. He was not, as I recall, particularly prone to public displays of affection – there wasn't a lot of him kissing or caressing her when we were all together. Yet whenever we were together, I was palpably aware that she meant everything to him.

Beyond that, he liked her very much. He also clearly thought that she was the most beautiful and desirable woman on the face of the earth.

One night the three of us were having dinner together at their apartment. (You've probably noticed by now that a lot of these stories involve meals. I'm struck by it myself, and I lived it.) Rosalie had left the dining room and was gone a while. "Where did Rosalie go?", I asked Edward. He didn't hear me, so his response was, "Who?"

"Your wife," I said, to which he replied, "Oh, you mean the dish?"

One of the reasons that I had spent so much time alone before we all became friends was that I always felt like the odd person out, a single woman in a world of couples. I didn't feel comfortable socializing with people in pairs. Because I was friends with each of them, for the most part I was comfortable being with them as a couple. On that night, among others, I felt a twinge of envy.

Well before I turned 30, I had decided that it would be impossible to find a man who would be everything I needed. I had been with men who were sexually attractive but with whom I found it hard to have a conversation. I had been with men who were good friends and a lot of fun to be with but were not interested in me sexually. I had been with men who wanted to have sex with me and cared nothing about my feelings or thoughts.

Edward and Rosalie were the ultimate couple. They loved each other, thoroughly enjoyed each other's company, found each other attractive, respected each other and were each other's best friends. I know that I didn't see all of their relationship, and I'm sure they must have argued or disagreed occasionally, but their connection was never in doubt.

They taught me that love, attraction, friendship and respect was possible in one relationship. They gave me hope and something to strive for, something I wouldn't find for years, but which was so worth the wait.

I uncovered an indiscretion involving french fries

Rosalie and I both have had food issues. (I still do – Rosalie has recently conquered hers.) It's the thing we share that we like about ourselves the least, although each of us is completely accepting of it in the other. Edward didn't get it.

This amazed us both, partially, I think, because Edward was very sensitive to most things, including women's issues in general and anything to do with Rosalie in particular. But he didn't get the food thing. To him, food was something you partake of when you feel hungry, push away when you've had enough, and that's it. He enjoyed good-tasting food, he appreciated the sensory pleasures good food offered, but he never really felt compelled to eat for any reason other than physical hunger.

(He was kind of like an alien to me in that way – like from another planet. Food is for comfort, right?)

This topic came up during a Thanksgiving dinner I attended at their house. There were only the three of us there. I was actively avoiding holidays with my family in those days, Edward's mother lived in Florida and Rosalie's family was, I suppose, otherwise occupied that year.

The evening was like many the three of us spent together – quiet, filled with laughter and good feelings and gratitude for the gifts our friendship provided. It was such a change from dinners with my family, which tended to be louder, more prone to family members talking about one another behind their backs, and me feeling like I needed to find a way to be invisible, as that was what I considered to be my place in our family.

Anyway, Rosalie and I were talking about liking turkey skin, and exchanging tales of trying to get more of it than is typically included in a serving or two of turkey. This all led to talk of other types of foods we liked and sometimes "had to have" whether we should have them or not. Edward was listening to us, but had nothing to contribute as he just didn't relate to it at all.

I lived alone and had been living alone for a number of years, so I was used to feeding whatever was in me asking for the wrong food whenever it reared its ugly head. There was no one to see me, to question why I was eating too much of the wrong things.

For Rosalie, it was different. She'd talk to Edward about wanting to lose weight or to look better, and, I think, based on my own experiences, she probably talked about foods she wanted to avoid. Then, when she really wanted one of those "off the list" foods, she found herself in a quandary – she couldn't suggest to Edward that they go get whatever she had sworn to eliminate from her diet. It would be akin to a recovering alcoholic asking her husband to take her out for a few drinks.

So, we were talking about food obsessions and compulsions, trading stories of our favorite "bad" foods, and in response to some confession of Rosalie's about her particular favorite, Edward said "I uncovered an indiscretion involving french fries just the other day."

It turned out that Rosalie had been in her old neighborhood and passed a hot dog stand that "always had the best french fries", and so of course she had to have some. So she bought them and ate them, and threw away the evidence, or so she thought. I guess Edward got into the car before it was fully aired out and recognized the distinctive aroma immediately, so the jig was up.

I laughed along with them at the retelling, and I felt for Rosalie, presuming she must have been embarrassed at being found out, as I knew I would have been. And yet I left there feeling a little sad, a little sorry for myself, and a little jealous of Rosalie, who had this man who loved her so much and so unconditionally that it never mattered to him what she weighed, what she ate, what her small weaknesses were.

Later, I realized that I needn't have felt jealous at all – Edward loved and accepted me as his friend, and it never mattered to him what I weighed, what I ate, or what my weaknesses were.

Are you sitting down?

A typical way, really, for Rosalie to begin a conversation. She sometimes enjoys being dramatic, I think, or perhaps she just has the ability to express what she's feeling more effectively than most people. In any case, when I heard the words, I didn't worry, I didn't wonder, I didn't panic – I just sat on the bed and then answered, "Yes."

In no way was I prepared to hear her next words, which were "Edward has a brain tumor." This conversation occurred in the winter of 1991, and I can still hear Rosalie saying those words in my head. I can see myself, pausing for a second, then saying urgently "Where are you?" She was at home, and I asked her if she wanted me to go over there. She said no.

Details, a few, started to emerge. Edward had been having some severe headaches and experiencing the sensation that his right hand was no longer connected to his body. After a few weeks, he went to the doctor. Rosalie said he was describing his symptoms to the doctor. When he got to the part about his hand, he said, speaking of the doctor, "That's when she got the worried look on her face."

Edward was sent to the hospital immediately, and a test identified a tumor. They admitted him then and there and scheduled surgery.

Suddenly, the word *surreal* meant something tangible to me. I just couldn't take it in. My first two thoughts in succession were "Edward is not going to live very long," and then "He'll be fine – they'll operate and it will be benign and he'll be fine." My two best defense mechanisms – expecting the worst and then denying the possibility that the worst can really happen.

Somehow through the fog of my own thoughts I realized that Rosalie was still talking. I heard her say "I'm sure he'd appreciate a visit," and I was so relieved to have something to do – I could go to the hospital the next day.

She ended the conversation after telling me she had other calls to make. I'm thinking I must have called my mother as soon as we hung up. I had some problems with my mother in my teens and early twenties, when I did not always think of her as the most supportive person in the world, but invariably, then as now, when something really bad (or really good) happened, I called my mother immediately.

I remember nothing of my conversation with her, and nothing more of that night. I do remember visiting Edward the next day, and thinking again how the surreal had replaced reality, and how living and breathing was like being in a nightmare. Edward couldn't be seriously ill, I

couldn't be sitting next to a hospital bed trying to think of things to talk about, and my God, he
couldn't possibly be having *brain surgery* the following morning.

    While I was there, Rosalie came in. She had gone home to get some things Edward needed, and she bustled in in her usual matter-of-fact way, talking about where she'd been and what she'd brought. She seemed unconcerned that her husband was lying in a hospital bed and that none of us knew what or how he would be when the surgery was over. She seemed **normal**.

    So much of Rosalie is inside of her. She must have been scared out of her mind that day, and that was my first glimpse of her coping mechanism – stay busy, focus on small things and you don't have to think about big things. If you don't talk about it, it won't happen.

When she had finished putting things away, Edward said something about there being some things they needed to talk about, and I knew that was my cue to leave. They were words that would have been mundane in any other context, but which sounded heartbreakingly important at that time and in that place.

I prepared to leave, afraid for Edward and Rosalie and sorry for myself, afraid of losing Edward – I had that luxury. Rosalie had to sit down and face her husband's mortality, and find a way to help him find the strength to survive and be healthy again. She had no time to be afraid or sorry for herself. I still don't know when she took that time, because she's never talked to me about it.

After I said my goodbyes, I walked out hearing him talking about life insurance policies, and the waking nightmare took residence in my brain.

Be nice to him, he has cancer

Edward is the first (and only) friend I have had who was diagnosed with a terminal illness. I did my best to "handle it" in the same way I have handled everything in my life – I did what I thought was right at any given point in time.

One day Edward and Rosalie showed up at my apartment for a dinner date and Edward, who had had a full head of hair when I had seen him a few days before, was completely bald. I was taken aback – I had realized that he might lose his hair, particularly since the cancer was in his brain – but the transformation was so quick and so complete that I was caught unawares. I believe I raised my eyebrows in surprise and said nothing, other than "hello."

Rosalie laughed a bit and said that Edward's hair had suddenly started coming out in handfuls, so they thought it would be better to just shave it off. Internally, I marveled at her ability to be so matter of fact about something that must have been very difficult for her. Outwardly, I gave Edward a once-over – he was wearing a turtleneck sweater and jeans, and was standing very straight. He looked very different, yet still himself. I said the first thing that came into my head, which was something like, "You look great in that sweater." He went to look at himself in a mirror and came back smiling.

    The evening was like a lot of our evenings together, food, conversation, laughter, love. I told him once that he looked like Yul Brynner, and he immediately put on his best King of Siam voice and said "One, two, three…"

    Another time I was kidding Edward about something. I have a sarcastic streak which I try to use for good -- I think I succeed most of the time. Anyway, I was teasing him or correcting some mistake he made, and Rosalie jokingly said, "Be nice to him – he has cancer."

For a split second I felt guilty – my dearest friend had a terminal illness and I was giving him a hard time. Then I realized that she had been joking. Cancer had become part of their lives. He had it, and they were living with it. There was no purpose in denying it or hiding from it, sweeping it under a rug or trying to create an illusion that it wasn't there.

Somehow they both found a strength that I had not been able to muster up. I knew in my head that Edward had cancer. I knew in my head that he would die too young. Yet I realized that night that I had never used the word "cancer" in their presence in any conversation that was not directly about his illness. I tried to compartmentalize it, I suppose. I tried to protect my heart from the inevitable outcome.

Again – I wanted to help Edward and Rosalie. I wanted to be a support for them, to make things easier for them. But again, and again and again, the opposite was true. They helped me accept Edward's illness as just another part of their lives – and mine.

Pregnant with twins!

Edward and Rosalie had a life plan. They got engaged, got married, and apparently made the decision to remain childless for a period of time. I never asked, and I'm not sure they would have told me had I asked, so I don't know if there was a specific time period they had in mind, or if they were waiting to get their careers to a certain point, or their bank balance to a specific level, or what. But clearly they had a plan.

Shortly after Edward was diagnosed, Rosalie and I were talking and she cheerily said that they had spoken to a doctor about freezing some of Edward's sperm in the event that after radiation, he could no longer have children.

That was one of the many times that I thought Rosalie was the bravest person on earth. I cannot conceive (no pun intended) of a scenario in which I would consider getting pregnant when my husband was so likely to have a less than impressive life expectancy. But, I learned, they had decided that this was the year they would begin trying to get pregnant, and they wanted to go ahead. So the sperm was frozen, and when the radiation was done, Rosalie began the in vitro fertilization process.

It took a little while. I think the first two rounds failed to produce a pregnancy. Rosalie was her usual in control, stoic self through all of this, at least with me. She dealt with the discomfort and the pressure and the disappointment when there was no pregnancy and she had to start over.

As soon as I was told that they were going to try in vitro, I immediately assumed they would have more than one baby, because I knew that the process involved the implanting of more than one fertilized egg.

I was sitting at my desk when Rosalie called with a report on the latest in vitro results. I answered the phone, she identified herself and I said, "How are you?" to which she replied in an excited voice, "Pregnant with twins!" I responded somehow, and she said I didn't seem surprised. I said I had been presuming all along that she would have more than one baby and she said no, it's very uncommon.

It was one of the conversations we had in which there was no mention or thought of cancer, of shortened life expectancy, or fear or worry. It was a few minutes of sheer bliss.

Being me, I knew that there would be days and weeks ahead that would not be so blissful. But I was blessed to have these wonderful friends who included me in their happiness that was strong enough to kick cancer to the curb for a time, and celebrate their lives and those to come.

I'm your friend

Here's the thing about me – for the most part, I'm a pretty reasonable person. I go out of my way to see both sides of every story and I believe that both sides have truth and value, even when I really want to be right. In my younger years, one of my major character flaws was that I thought I could fix conflict by inserting myself into the middle of it.

My nephew Nathan developed a seizure disorder early in 1991, when he was seven months old. In the beginning everyone thought it was not a huge deal, perhaps even a one-time occurrence. We learned quickly how wrong we were. Nathan tolerated dozens, if not hundreds, of seizures every day.

It's hard to put into words what Nathan's illness did to my family. For those of us in the Chicago area, it was a nightmare made both easier and harder by distance. For my brother Howard, my sister-in-law Susan and my nephew Benjamin, the impact was different for each of them. Susan was a tower of strength and was there to do whatever Nathan needed. Benjamin, who was three when Nathan was born, learned to accept the attention deficits that come with having a sick sibling. And Howard – Howard found himself needing support, perhaps more than at any other time in his life.

Howard has always held a very special place in our family. He is my parents' firstborn and the first grandchild. While I've always loved him (even during the birth through high school years when his sole purpose in life seemed to be to ignore and/or torment me) I've also always resented him in some ways. He gets that – he realizes his position in the family and what that means for me – to the extent that he once referred to himself in a conversation with me as "the golden boy."

After leaving home to attend college in Iowa in 1975, Howard never lived in the Chicago area again. When he got his Bachelor's degree, he went on the graduate school at Washington University in Saint Louis and he has lived in Saint Louis ever since.

He likes being close enough to visit or receive visitors without being too close. He likes his life in Saint Louis. He met Susan there and they've been married over 25 years. My point here is that Howard didn't really look to us, the family he grew up with, for emotional support.

Somewhat to his own surprise, I think, that changed during Nathan's illness. My mother stayed in close touch, I stayed in closer touch than usual, and other family members stepped up to do what they could. My father was a notable exception.

At that time, my father was living in a rented apartment in a suburb of Chicago while his second wife and her children were living in Florida. I had dinner with him one evening and we got to talking about family stuff, and he told me in a very pained voice that, "due to circumstances I cannot disclose to you, I am convinced that your brother wants nothing to do with me." Or words to that effect. He wouldn't talk about it any further and told me that under no circumstances was I to repeat any of the conversation to Howard.

As it happened, I talked to Howard the next day, really not intending to say a word about Dad's thoughts. But in the course of my conversation with Howard, he started talking about how confused he was that Dad was not in touch, and how he really needed all the support he could get at that time.

You can see where this is going, right? It seemed so clear cut at the time. Both of them were in pain thinking the other didn't care about them, and I could fix it all with a few sentences. So I told Howard what my father had told me and asked him not to let my dad know.

Howard wrote my father a letter in which he actually quoted verbatim some of what I had said, so of course my father knew I had broken his confidence. At that time, my father was pretty much all I had in terms of emotional support. I was trying hard to take care of Edward and Rosalie, be there for my mother, be there for Howard – and no one was there for me, because everyone was worried about someone else.

When my father called me, furious that I had not kept silent, I just lost it. After Dad hung up on me, I called Howard and got an answering machine. I left a very long message during which I was crying uncontrollably and telling him that he'd taken my father away from me and a lot more that I'm just as happy I can't remember any more.

When he heard the message, he called me in an absolute fury and told me he never wanted to speak to me or hear from me again, and I lost it all over again.

To this day, nineteen years later, I still refer to this incident as the only thing I've ever done in my life of which I am truly ashamed.

Shortly after this took place, Edward stopped by for some reason. I was not in good enough shape to be described as a mess. I poured out the whole story – I still wonder how much of it he understood – I was crying so hard – and when I'd finished I started going on about how I was a terrible person and nobody could ever care about me.

He just moved closer, put his arms around me, and said very quietly, "I'm your friend. I love you."

I miss him so much.

We tried to think of a way to have you be a godmother....

Rosalie said that to me, in the girls' bedroom where she was nursing one of them during the party after their christening. It hit a nerve – a bunch of nerves, in fact.

In my family, godparent in an honorary title, bestowed upon someone special to one or both parents, and nothing more. There is no religious significance attached to their role in a child's life. I don't know if this is a Jewish thing or just a thing in my family, where, as I've said, religion is not that big a priority.

I had hugely mixed feelings when Rosalie became pregnant. I was thrilled for her and Edward, who I knew had always planned to have children. I was nervous that a baby would somehow make me less important to them, that they would only want friends who also had children. I was in awe of Rosalie's bravery, making a careful, thoughtful decision to get pregnant knowing her husband's prognosis. I was jealous, because I have always wanted children and always felt some jealousy when someone else was having a baby. I was happy that some tangible part of Edward would live on, whatever happened to him and when. I was scared, for both of them.

And I knew that none of my feelings mattered – I just wanted to be there for them, to help them prepare, to enjoy the pregnancy with them to whatever degree I was allowed to do so, and to have a close, loving attachment to what turned out to be two beautiful baby girls.

I did what I could for the 9 months – most of the doing seemed to be near the end of the pregnancy. I spent countless hours cross-stitching two samplers – one with the alphabet and one with numbers – for the babies' room, and took them to be framed. I believe I helped put baby furniture together, which is definitely not my strong suit. I hosted a baby shower in my apartment, which came with its own angst, as I had told Rosalie she could invite whomever she liked, and at the last minute she wanted to invite a woman who she and Edward did not like, who I could not stand, because a friend of Edward's had said the woman would be hurt if she were not invited. I bought 4 christening outfits – 2 for girls and 2 for boys, so they'd be prepared for any combination of genders. And I was just there, it seems in retrospect, a lot.

Rosalie seemed to enjoy her pregnancy, despite the (I've been told) normal inconveniences like trouble sleeping and swollen ankles. She seemed to enjoy the prospect of not working, too, which really surprised me. I had always taken for granted that Rosalie loved her work and that it was a priority for her – perhaps I only thought that because I am pretty much that way and I just took for granted that she would feel the same.

Anyway, I remember the pregnancy as a good period for them both. Edward was still working and holding good thoughts about beating cancer and the odds, and they were both looking so forward to being parents. I enjoyed being able to share the anticipation with them.

Hayley and Claire were born in 1992. By that time, I felt that Edward and Rosalie and I were very close, and I thought that I would be the girls' godmother, or at least godmother to one of them. Had I known that in Christian faiths, godparents are supposed to help ensure that children receive proper religious training, I would have known better. But early in the pregnancy I didn't know, and even when I found out, I still thought they would ask me.

There was a television show on in those years, called *Life Goes On*. The show centered around a teenager with Down's Syndrome, growing up in a Catholic family with a couple of sisters, also teens. That year, the mother became pregnant and she and her husband struggled over who to name as godparents. She ended up asking her Jewish boss, because it was an honor they wanted to bestow on him and they knew he would respect the role and honor his commitment to the child. It was from that show that I learned the traditional role godparents play, and because of the outcome of the episode, I continued to hope that I would be asked.

I wasn't. They never brought up the subject, and I was never able to ask casually who they were going to have as godparents because it meant so much to me. Shortly before the christening, I learned that Rosalie's stepmother Marge and another friend, Carol, would be godmothers.

Even knowing why I hadn't been asked, I was hurt. It was a hard day for me, being there and not feeling part of anything – just a guest. It seemed that Marge was trying deliberately to rub my Jewish nose in the fact that I had been excluded by talking about the *Life Goes On* episode – I don't know what her point was in bringing it up, but it seemed like she was saying, "See, they could have asked you even though you're Jewish, but you're not important enough."

Petty? Sure. Unreasonable? Of course. But I'm human. I loved them both, I felt so connected to them and to the girls even before they were born, and I was denied the recognition that I was special to them.

The afternoon wore on, and at some point I wandered into the nursery where Rosalie was nursing one of the twins, and while we were in there, she said "Did I tell you before that we tried to think of a way to have you be a godmother?" I said no, she hadn't mentioned it, and she talked on about how they really wanted me to do it, but it just didn't seem possible.

I don't know if she could tell that I was hurt or not. I'm not good about hiding my feelings. Anyway, beyond my feelings for Rosalie's stepmother, about whom I could never feel good again, the whole incident changed nothing.

I love Hayley and Claire with all my heart, I continued to love Edward and Rosalie and to spend a lot of time with them, and I continued to feel special to them all.

What I learned from the whole thing was that I could be hurt by those I loved and still feel love for them and from them. Relationships have always been murky things to me, and I had learned at a young age that love can be withdrawn with one false move.

I learned that you don't always get everything you want from a relationship, and that things don't happen just because you expect them to. I learned that whatever disappointments there might be, the love and friendship are always there.

I thank God for you every day, Rosalie.

I spoke those words, in a Chicago alley, to my friend Rosalie one day in the summer of 1993. We were walking from my apartment to hers, a block away. The night before, my apartment building had caught fire. I had been trapped in my apartment for a short time and, due to smoke inhalation, had to spend the night in intensive care.

Rosalie spent much of that night carting a red wagon between her place and my third-floor walkup apartment – the firemen chopped in a back door to get in to my unit and several windows were broken, so the building and my belongings were not secure, including the computer equipment I needed to operate the consulting business I had started two months before. She took everything that seemed important from my smoky apartment, walking around broken glass and other debris, and rolled it down the stairs and over to her building where she knew it would be safe.

(When she entered my apartment, she saw a cardboard box sitting in the front hall. She had no idea what it was, but because of the location in which it was found, it seemed important, so she took it with her. I had brought the box upstairs with me when I came home shortly before the fire started. It contained thousands of 3 X 5 cards on which were recorded 30 years of gift histories for the donors of a convent which had hired me to create computer records of the information. Essentially, Rosalie saved my business that night.)

She also found time to contact the hospital to check on me, call my mother and other people to let them know I was all right, find a place in her apartment to lock up my cats, and collect some clothes to bring me the following day, so I wouldn't have to leave the hospital in a smoky nightgown.

The next morning she came to my hospital room, waited while I dressed, brought me to my apartment so I could see for myself that it was completely unlivable. Then we walked to her place to get my cats, so I could take my brood to my mother's house until the apartment was habitable.

The fact that she did all this, without question, without being asked, amazed me in and of itself. When you add to that the fact that she had at home twin girls, aged 8 months, and a husband who was ill and became so upset when he realized my building was on fire that he had a seizure, it becomes a gift of almost mythic proportion.

Leaving her apartment with my cats in hand, I remembered that day years before when I had first seen

Rosalie, and thought she didn't seem like the nicest person I'd ever met. I couldn't believe I had ever felt that way, however briefly. Then I remembered the Personal Pac mission, and that once I had spent five minutes talking to her, she felt like part of me. I thought again that I might never have taken the time to get to know Rosalie if she had not been with Edward, and how Rosalie's love and friendship had sustained me in so many ways.

Comfort food

Throughout the 3 ½ years from his diagnosis until his death, Edward battled cancer with a quiet courage and a grace that I know I would not be able to manage in his place. I always knew that there must be turmoil within – I knew that he must be frightened and sad and angry and aching for his family.

For most of their marriage, Edward and Rosalie lived on the third floor of a condo building. It was a converted apartment building that had no central air conditioning. Their unit also had no window air conditioners. Most of the windows were long and very narrow, not made with air conditioners in mind. Both Rosalie and Edward were pretty stoic about the Chicago summers, but days that were over 90 were pretty hard to deal with.

During the summer of 1993, when Hayley and Claire were about 10 months old, Edward's mother Elsie was in town from her home in Florida and staying with Edward and Rosalie. Rosalie's mother Roseann was also visiting during one of the weekends that Elsie was in town. I called on one of the weekend mornings and suggested that perhaps they might like to go out to a mall or someplace that would be cool, and since they would not all fit in one car I could come along and drive some of them in my car, which was air conditioned.

Eventually the suggestion was adopted and I drove Edward and Roseann or Elsie in my car, while Rosalie drove their car with the other mother and the twins. I had recently bought a Billy Joel album, River of Dreams, and there was a song on it that I wanted Edward to hear. It was a lullaby for Joel's daughter Alexa, and I knew that he would find a message for his daughters in the lyrics:

I played the song in my car as we were driving toward the mall. By the time the song ended, Edward was quietly sobbing in his seat next to me. I knew the song would affect him, but I was a little taken aback at the depth of his reaction.

During the drive, we had stopped at an intersection where volunteers were collecting coins for a charity. I had put some money in the can and been given a small Tootsie Roll as a thank you. I had the candy in my pocket and as I was watching Edward's reaction to the song, I tossed it into his lap and said, "Comfort food."

The words and the surprise of having the candy appear so suddenly did the trick. Edward laughed, wiped his face and was himself again.

He was the bravest person I will ever know.

I want my children to grow up knowing good people

For as long as he could after he became ill, Edward worked at Children's Home and Aid Society of Illinois. He went there after leaving Planned Parenthood, having accepted the fact that there was no career path for him to become either Executive Director or a fund raiser.

However misguided he might have been when he took what was essentially a secretarial position at Planned Parenthood hoping it would lead to much bigger things, he did far better in his next endeavor. He started at CHASI as the staff person who supported the Women's Auxiliary, which is a position often considered fairly low on the fundraising totem pole.

Women's auxiliaries often do wonderful work for the organizations they serve. The women are dedicated, tireless volunteers committed to the mission of the organization. They can raise a great deal of money. As someone who has been connected to fundraising for over 25 years, I must honestly say that I admire the women who choose to volunteer their time and energy in this way.

However, it must be stressed that these women are volunteers, and working with volunteers is something that not everyone can do. Auxiliary members frequently expect a great deal of support from what is usually an already-overburdened staff, and staff members must be able to either provide the support in as seamless a fashion as possible, or be able to explain to someone who is not being paid to do anything why they will have to do it themselves.

The CHASI Auxiliary put on a gala dinner every year. As is typical for this type of event, there is a tremendous amount of planning, coordination, scheduling, juggling and money involved. The CHASI women worked extremely hard all year to benefit the organization and be sure that they made it money. They demanded a lot from the staff, and they gave a lot in return.

Edward loved them all. He got to know each person individually and as far as I know, they all loved him in return. He did what they needed him to do. He worked hard at working hard – not only putting in the hours required and providing the services demanded, but doing it all with a consistent good nature, respect for even the most difficult volunteer, and his usual quiet commitment to excellence.

He worked with the Auxiliary for two or three years and then (to the dismay of many of the Auxiliary members) began moving up the ladder in the Development Department. He used to talk to me from time to time about what he felt were his deficiencies. He needed to learn a lot of new things and while he embraced every challenge, he was sometimes worried about not being able to measure up.

I would take each conversation as it came and offer suggestions if I had any, or just listen and make reassuring comments if I didn't. In truth, I'm not sure he had deficiencies. He was a natural fundraiser. He believed wholeheartedly in the work CHASI was doing and he wanted to raise money to help them do it. He could work to accomplish this goal via writing, personal visits, events – whatever was needed.

Ultimately he was promoted to Director of Development. In typical Edward fashion, he felt bad about the fact that this happened due to a misfortune that befell his predecessor. I felt bad about the misfortune too – I had heard a lot about it as things developed – but I knew that Edward had been working toward this for a long time and I was thrilled for him that finally, hard work had been its own reward for him. He LOVED his job.

After I started my business, we spoke less frequently during the day. I was working at client sites and trying very hard to keep enough money coming in so that I would not have to get a "real" job or file for unemployment.

When I had clients to see downtown, I would try to find a way to see Edward as well. Sometimes I would drive to his office at the end of my day and wait for the end of his day so I could give him a ride home. Sometimes we would go out to lunch together, I think, or I would drop him off in the morning.

As his illness progressed, his moods sometimes changed quickly. One on occasion, after a light-hearted drive from somewhere to his office, he began talking about how important it was to him that I stay close to Rosalie and the girls. He looked at me and said quietly, "I want my children to grow up knowing good people."

I could see in his eyes that he was depending on me – to be there for Rosalie, to be someone Hayley and Claire could love and respect and learn from. I promised him I would be there.

It's one of the ways in which I failed Edward – I was not there. I let first my business, and later my marriage, keep me away. Hayley and Claire grew up, I think, knowing I was important to Rosalie and probably that I was important to Edward, but, I fear, not understanding how desperately I wished that I was important to them.

I allowed myself to be relegated to the "emergency contact", to the very occasional visit. I didn't know how to put my marriage first and still remain present in the world I had inhabited before I was married.

I will feel guilty about this for the rest of my life. While I believe that Edward understands and has forgiven me, I let him down. I broke a promise. I know that Edward would want me to forgive myself, but I don't know how.

Do you believe in heaven?

Edward and I had some wonderful, long, philosophical discussions over the years. When he left Planned Parenthood before I did, to work at Children's Home and Aid Society of Illinois, we were both working in fundraising, so we would talk about that. We'd talk about families, friends, relationships, our childhood experiences..... whatever came up.

Once I was in my car driving home from some work appointment, and there was a big crash on the expressway so I had to get off and I found I was in an unfamiliar and not very safe-looking neighborhood. I was very nervous about being alone, so I called Edward from the car and we talked about anything and everything till I was safely home. I loved those talks.

During one of them, we were building castles in the air. I was working at Metafile Information Systems, the job I took when I left Planned Parenthood in 1987. Edward was at Children's Home and Aid, and at the time things were a bit rough there, with some staff shakeups.

Both of us actually loved our jobs at that point, but we each enjoyed being fanciful on occasion, and on this occasion I suggested that we open a consulting firm together someday. We could build some sort of bridge from my third floor apartment to his, so that clients could easily get from one of us to the other. Edward would consult with clients about their fundraising needs and I would consult about their software needs. We wanted Rosalie to be part of the firm, of course, although as a gynecological nurse practitioner, her skills were in a somewhat different direction. Rosalie, Edward said, would provide the female clients with a pap smear.

After he became ill, he would often talk with me about his illness, his fears about leaving his family and his concern for their welfare after he was gone. When the twins were first born, Rosalie signed him up for a parenting class at a local community college. It might have been a little later, when he had to stop working and stay home to care for them while she went back to work. In any case, the class met at night, and he was no longer able to drive by then, because he occasionally had seizures. I volunteered to take him to and/or pick him up from the class.

On one of those nights, he talked about how much he wanted to be around when Hayley and Claire were older. As we talked, he got off on a tangent about how dangerous it was for kids to be with other kids, where they can be exposed to drugs, sex too early, encouraged by their peers to do the wrong thing, etc. He was thinking about home schooling, I believe. As we neared the school where his class was being held. I tried to end on a light note by reminding him that as yet, his children could not even crawl, so he had little reason to fear that he'd lose them to the streets any time soon.

Another time on the phone..... Edward was not doing that well. His tumor has recurred and he had had a second surgery; he had suffered some seizures and he was less able to express himself verbally or on paper. He also seemed to react to things much more slowly. He had had to stop working, as he had lost some capabilities that made it impossible for him to successfully work as a fundraiser. He was put on medical disability and he stayed home taking care of Hayley and Claire while Rosalie went to work full time.

This was a very tough transition for them both. Rosalie had wanted to stay home with the girls for a couple of years at least, and Edward loved his work and wanted to be well enough to provide for his family and to continue to contribute to society.

My own schedule was kind of spotty that year. Since 1987, I had been working for Metafile, a company that sold fund raising software. It was a perfect fit for me until 1992. My manager, Joyce, who became a good friend, left near the end of that year, and the owner of the company called to fire me, saying without Joyce they had no need for a local account manager, they would move my job to Rochester, Minnesota, where the company was based, and replace me with a person on staff in Rochester.

I talked him into keeping me on in a sales role. I had been selling the software for a year or so, which was not the worst thing I was ever asked to do for money, but I don't really like sales. I enjoy providing service to people, a role in which I feel that I contribute to the work of the nonprofit community by helping fundraisers do what they need to do. Anyway, Allan agreed that I could continue to be employed as long as I averaged one sale per month, which would cover the cost of my employment.

At the end of 1992, we closed the local office in Lombard and I moved a little furniture, a copy machine, my computer, printer, fax machine and files into my mother's basement. I had to have a home to work out of, and my apartment was too small.

Ostensibly, I went to my mother's each day to make cold calls to people to try to interest them in the software. In fact, I spent a lot of time there playing computer games, returning calls and scheduling appointments. One sale a month was not that hard, and the arrangement I had made with the company president was that all I needed was an *average* of one sale per month, so if I got two sales in one month and none the next, I'd still be fine.

I closed one sale in January and one in February. In March, I closed 2 sales. In April, I was not able to close a sale. Before I could even get the paperwork faxed in on the 1st, Allan called to say that since I had not closed a sale in April, as per our agreement I was being terminated. I reminded him of the actual terms of our agreement, and he said, okay, then, I'd be able to stay on. As soon as he told me I still had a job, I quit. During the two week notice period, I sent a mailing to all the customers in our area, telling them I was leaving and would be available for independent projects if they needed anything. I picked up some work trying to design an application in dBase (about which I knew nothing.) I lined up as many job interviews as I could. I got a couple of offers, but nothing that felt remotely good to me.

As of May 15th, I was officially unemployed. I had enough money to live on for six weeks, so I decided not to apply for unemployment benefits right away and to use the six weeks to try to generate enough income on my own to pay the bills. I was told I had an 18-month period during which I could file for unemployment and still get my full benefits, and decided I might as well take a shot at self-employment before I gave up and took a "real job."

In those first couple of months, I wasn't that busy, but I still had money coming in from the old job and a little breathing room to generate some work, which thankfully (and amazingly, since I really had no clue what I was doing) I was able to do. As I write this in 2010, I still have not had to claim those unemployment benefits. Along the way I've incorporated my business had a couple of employees and several contractors – it's possible that this is my real job.

The very early days of this endeavor were nervous but relatively stress-free. I had some time to myself and time for Edward and Rosalie. And so it was that I found myself on the phone one evening, talking with Edward while Rosalie was out.

He asked me if I believed in heaven.

In part, he asked me as a Jewish person – he did not know if Jews believe in heaven or an afterlife, and when the question came up, I realized that I didn't know either. We had a theological/philosophical sort of conversation, and I closed it by saying – because I didn't know what to say other than what I felt – "I don't know what happens to us when we die. All I know is that wherever you are, you'll always be with me."

I didn't realize how true the words were until I heard myself say them, but that sentence was one of the fundamental truths that periodically present themselves to us. The people that we love are always with us.

After my conversation with Edward, I bought some books about the Jewish religion and in one, I found a reference to *olam ha-ba*, or afterlife. It says that the Torah does not mention an afterlife, possibly out of a desire to ensure that Judaism not evolve in the direction of the Egyptian religion. But, it says, "In Judaism, the belief in afterlife is less a leap of faith than a logical outgrowth of other Jewish beliefs. If one believes in a God who is all-powerful and all-just, one cannot believe that this world, in which evil far too often triumphs, is the only arena in which human life exists."

Some suggestions about afterlife in Jewish folklore are humorous, or at least attempting to be humorous. One story teaches that in heaven, Moses sits and teaches Torah all day long. For some people, this is heaven. For others, it's hell.

Judaism encourages us to leave the afterlife in God's hands. It comforts me to believe that God is taking care of those that we have lost. And I hang onto the idea of heaven. I still feel Edward's presence, just as I still see him whenever I look into Claire or Hayley's face. I think of him nearly every day, and of everything he gave me.

I was able to give something to Edward that day. When I told him that he'd always be with me, he thanked me and began to cry. I know he had been feeling that he would be gone and lost in some way, as though he had never been here, as though his presence here had not mattered. I thank God for giving me those words to give to him at that time, when he needed to hear them so badly.

Yet as always, Edward gave me more. That day became part of my own spiritual growth, as it prompted me to search for answers from Judaism, something I had never done before. It helped define me. And what a gift it was, to be able to provide comfort to someone who had so often comforted and sustained me.

Donny Osmond? You're kidding, right?

In 1993 or 1994, a production of *Joseph and the Amazing Technicolor Dreamcoat* came to Chicago and settled in. I knew it was in town, but my business was pretty young, my 22-month old nephew Nathan had recently died of complications from a seizure disorder, and my best friend was fighting brain cancer. I didn't go.

One of my clients went to see the show and we chatted about it during one of my visits. She had loved it and thought I would enjoy it. I confess I had been wanting to go, because I have always had an affinity for Donny Osmond, who was starring in the show as Joseph. The reason for the affinity (other than the fact that he was adorable, of course) is that I learned from some teen magazine that Donny and I had both been born on December 9th, 1957.

Anyway, I invited someone to go with me, got two tickets and went to see the show. It's a stretch to say that it changed my life, but it certainly made a huge difference in my life at that time. During a period where so many bad things were happening, *Joseph* was bright colors, bright lights, great energy, light-hearted, and **FUN**.

That show became my salvation until it left town, many months later. I saw it more than 20 times, often alone. It was my escape and my way to recharge my batteries so I could keep on working, keep on being wherever Edward and Rosalie needed me to be, keep on finding ways to keep on.

Something in me knew that Rosalie would scoff at the idea of Donny Osmond – we were of an age where he seemed very much in our past – but I really wanted both of them to see the show. I brought it up a couple of times (the first time her response was "Donny Osmond? You're kidding, right?), but I stuck to my guns and finally she agreed that we would go. I got tickets about 6 rows from the stage, center section (we could see the scar on Donny's stomach).

Sitting next to Edward in the theater that day, I was a little worried because one of the outcomes of his surgeries was that he became somewhat prone to seizures, and the show included some strobe lighting. I had mentioned that before getting the tickets, and they said they thought it would be okay.

The show started and I got caught up in it as I always did. I'm sure we must have chatted during intermission, but I don't remember what we talked about at all. What I remember is the end of the show.

I remember looking to my left and seeing Edward, his hands above his head, fists clenched. He was cheering and whistling, and smiling, and somehow I felt that for the previous two hours, he had escaped cancer.

If that's true, I believe that giving Edward those two hours may be the most important thing I will ever do.

When can you babysit?

Edward was diagnosed in February of 1991 and battled cancer with everything he had for three and a half years. During this time, my life was very closely connected to Edward and Rosalie and, when they arrived in 1992, Hayley and Claire. By choice, I made myself available to them all as much as I could, whenever I could, for as long as I could.

Naturally, I had other things going on. I had a job that kept me busy during the week. I had my family. Nathan died in April of 1992 a couple of months shy of his second birthday. I went with my mother to the funeral.

My brother and his family live 300 miles from Chicago. I don't see very much of them, just due to calendars, mostly. But I really had wanted to be a good aunt to Nathan and Benjamin. I wasn't, but I don't think they missed me. There's a very lot of family in our family, with divorces and remarriages on both sides. When Benjamin was born, he had 4 grandmothers, 2 grandfathers, 3 great-grandmothers and 1 great-grandfather. Technically I suppose that he had 3 grandfathers, because my mother was married to her second husband Jerry when Benjamin was born, but he walked out on her when she got home from Nathan's funeral. Jerry is the only person on the planet that I knew personally and absolutely hated. I would still hate him today if I ever gave him a thought. Okay, I do occasionally give him a thought, and I still hate him.

I had offered to baby-sit for Hayley and Claire on a few occasions. I was happy to do it – they were sweet babies and I knew it was good for Edward and Rosalie to be able to get out together. But I had kind of burned myself with babysitting in my twenties. I had a friend at the first real full-time job I ever had, Art Azen. His wife had a baby during the time Art and I worked at the same place, and I impulsively offered to baby-sit when the baby was born. I did a lot of baby-sitting in my teens, and I liked it, but I really never expected them to take me up on it. However, they did. I first sat with Stephanie when she was just a few weeks old, and I spent nearly every Saturday night, first with her, then with her and her brother Michael, for about 8 years. By that time, I realized that I had no dating life, and if something didn't change in my life, I would die a childless old maid because I was on some level thinking of Michael and Stephanie as my children. I've recently reconnected with both of them, and to be honest, I still kind of think of them as partly mine.

So – while I was happy to help Edward and Rosalie with the twins, I wasn't so excited about the idea of babysitting. I think there were a few times that they asked me and I said I couldn't do it for one reason or another. This always made me feel extremely guilty, but I would tell myself that I had done a lot for Edward and Rosalie, and I was entitled to some time to myself, blah blah blah…

While I was busy rationalizing what was essentially nothing but selfishness on my part, Edward's health was deteriorating. Finally Rosalie called me one evening and, after the preliminary hellos, just said bluntly "When can you baby-sit?"

There was a tiny hint of desperation in her voice that just broke my heart. I had recognized my need to have some time for myself, but in doing so I had ignored her need to be with Edward, just the two of them. Not my finest hour.

And so we set a date. I arrived at the requested time and sat in the living room talking with Edward while Rosalie was getting ready. I think it was this evening that

Edward began speaking of some controversial treatment that was available somewhere outside of the United States. He was considering going away for the treatment.

I didn't think it was a good idea, and I told him that. I've wondered about that a lot. My thoughts at the time were that he should be spending every available moment with Rosalie and the twins because no matter what he did, there were only going to be so many moments left. A tumor as aggressive as his turned out to be was not likely to be defeated with a new treatment. How could he plan to be away alone, on another continent?

I basically said that at some point, he was going to have to accept that taking extraordinary steps to try to live longer could cost him more viable time with his family than he could get from taking the steps.

Whether it was because of anything I said or not, there was no experimental treatment. He stayed in Chicago, with his family. And he and Rosalie had one last night out alone together.

He's not going anywhere

For most of the time that I knew them, Edward and Rosalie lived in a condo in a converted rental apartment building. Like me, they lived on the third floor of a three-story building with no elevator and no central air-conditioning. The apartment was perfectly fine for them until Edward got sick.

At first small things within the apartment became somewhat problematic. For example, in an age where everyone in the world seemed to be using push-button phones, Edward and Rosalie had the old, heavy rotary dial phones. We all loved those phones (I had push-buttons at home, but I kind of coveted the rotary phones) but after Edward's first surgery, it became hard for him to use them. His memory had been affected by the surgery and he would forget who he was calling, or how many of the numbers he had already dialed, while waiting for the dial to reset itself.

I would see or hear about these small things and try to shrug them off – part of the defense mechanism at work. Early on in Edward's illness, there were things that would happen that I would opt to see as temporary – a result of the tumor that had been removed, or something that he would find a way to work around somehow. The phone thing was one of those things. In fact, in the end Rosalie switched to push-button phones.

I could see changes in Edward throughout the course of his illness. His vision was affected in the first surgery, I think, but he did find a way to compensate for that. After his third surgery his voice and/or his hearing was affected. He began speaking so softly that it was nearly impossible to hear him. It annoyed me when I first spent time with him struggling to hear a word he said, but Rosalie explained the situation and I tried to get used to that as another one of those things.

Along the way, I came to the realization that I was using all these things as some kind of leverage. Okay, so Edward can't dial a phone – he's here. He can't modulate the volume of his speech – so what? He's here. I can deal with these things – just keep him here.

After the third surgery, the doctors said they would not be able to operate again. And I think radiation was also off the table, so there was little else they could do to prolong Edward's life. He went into the hospital one more time, I think, for some kind of intense chemo treatment.

When he left the hospital, he was very weak and tired. Rosalie called once they were home and settled. While I am not, in general, an idiot, for some reason in the course of the conversation I asked her if they would want to go out. Her response was immediate and firm: "He's not going anywhere." Apparently it had taken a **very** long time to get Edward up three flights of stairs and settled in.

There had been some talk about them taking a trip to Washington, where Rosalie's brother and his family lived. Suddenly the plans were changed. Edward wanted to see Mike, Valerie and their daughters, but Rosalie bought them all plane tickets and they came to Chicago. When I asked Edward about the sudden change in plans, he said "I don't want to be that far away from my undertaker."

He didn't leave the apartment again until Rosalie called the funeral home to come and pick him up. (Rosalie's sense of irony might have helped keep her grounded on what I have to believe was the worst night of her life. The funeral home said someone would be there in about 45 minutes, and as she hung up, her mother heard her mutter under her breath "Just like a pizza…")

During his last days, Edward stayed in the living room, in a rented hospital bed. His daughters were walking by then – they were a few months shy of their second birthday – and Claire, who looks very much like Edward, would sometimes crawl into his bed and curl up in the crook of his arm and nap with him.

Various friends and family came and went. He spoke with people as best as he could while he was awake, dozed frequently, and began slipping very quietly away.

See if you can find a female minister

I spent most of the last day of Edward's life with Rosalie. He was peacefully asleep in his hospital bed in the living room. I wanted so badly to be able to do something that I have the feeling that I virtually *begged* Rosalie to let me go with her to run some "unpleasant errands", as she put it.

Most of what we did was shop for a dress for her to wear to Edward's funeral. How incredibly surreal it is, to be calmly watching one of your closest friends trying on dresses – looking for one that was inexpensive because she knew she would never want to wear it again – while her husband and the man who has been like a brother to you for 10 years is dying a few miles away.

I remember thinking what vastly different meanings there are in the word "dying." For years I had told myself that Edward was dying, in the sense that he had a serious illness from which he would almost certainly die. Yet suddenly he was literally dying – life was ebbing from him as he lay in his home, surrounded by those who loved him.

His voice had left him the day before. Somehow he lost the ability to make sounds, and he seemed frustrated and slightly panicked, which is not surprising, since I'm sure he had many things he wanted to be able to say.

From then on he seemed less and less present. And so we went on with the day while he lay there, peacefully asleep. And I went with Rosalie while she picked out a dress, and talked quietly with her in the car about nothing – what was there to talk about? And I went back to her apartment with her and I had dinner with her and the girls and her mother and Edward's mother, and I think a number of other people. Finally I had to go home – I had no other reason to be in the apartment. I looked in on Edward on my way out – he remained peacefully asleep.

The phone rang early the next morning. I knew who it was, and I knew what it meant, and never in my life have I so dreaded answering a telephone. An exchange of hellos, and then two words, very quietly spoken: "He's gone."

I found I couldn't focus on feeling anything – I wanted to be able to be happy that Edward was not in pain anymore; I knew that I would be grieving for my own loss for a long time to come, once I began to feel it; I knew that my heart would ache for Hayley and Claire and the loss they would feel all of their lives without knowing they were feeling it; and I knew that I could never even imagine what Rosalie was feeling. Even now that I am married I can't fathom that kind of loss. The magnitude of losing my husband Larry is more than I can bring myself to intellectualize about – I don't know how a person lives through that.

I couldn't feel any of that right at that moment, so I asked if there was anything I could do for Rosalie. She said yes, she had made most of the arrangements for the funeral, but Edward had told her that he wanted a female minister of their faith to officiate and she didn't know where to find one. "See if you can find a female minister," she told me.

Somehow a female minister was found – I don't remember now whether I found her or not. I contacted a man from one of my faith-based client sites and told him what I needed, and I think he made some calls and found a few women. But it's possible that the woman who did the service was actually found by someone else.

What I remember about this is not the fact that a woman was found or how; but rather why we were looking for one. Edward read a newspaper article a few weeks before he died from which he learned that his faith made it extremely difficult for women to become ministers and serve as such in the churches. He was outraged. It appalled him that any church, particularly his own, would exclude women from serving in the capacity for which they had been trained and dedicated their lives. He read the article in a hospital room, where he was undergoing the last "last ditch effort" the doctors could come up with to prolong his life. Since he clearly was not going to be in a position to crusade for the rights of women in his faith, he decided to make his point the only way he could.

And so he told Rosalie that he wanted a woman to officiate at his funeral. Without question, she agreed and she made it happen. She did everything he wanted – they must have spent a long time discussing everything. They wrote his obituary together, they planned the funeral, they talked about how she would sing the girls to sleep each night when he was gone.

We were only partially successful. We found the minister, but Edward's church would not allow her to perform the service in the church, so we had to compromise – the woman would conduct a service at the funeral home, and there would be another service at the church afterward.

I remember little of the funeral home service. It's the only time in my life I've actually "felt numb". I've always thought that a senseless phrase, since if you're numb you can't feel at all. Yet I was so conscious of not feeling anything – of not *being able* to feel anything – that I could only feel the nothingness.

It seemed surreal to me – Edward's body laid out in a casket surprised me, as I knew he was going to be cremated. Jewish funerals typically do not include open caskets, so I had never seen a deceased person laid out before that day. I've seen corpses since who looked nothing like they did in life – but Edward looked just exactly like Edward, dressed up in a suit one last time.

Only Edward could continue to fight, quietly, with dignity and determination for what he believed to be right, even after his life was over. Only Edward could have had such a generosity of spirit that he would use his own funeral to correct an injustice in whatever way he could. Only Edward could give me the gift of knowing that no matter how sad or lost you are, there are things to be fought for; things to be fixed; things to be made right. And that small victories may or may not eventually win the war, but those not attempted will surely lose it.

Here's a bus token

Edward was compassionate from birth, I think. By the time I met him when he was about 30, compassion came so naturally to him that I couldn't imagine him ever having been without it.

Cancer increased his emotional reactions at some point. After he died, Rosalie met with the pastor or whoever would give Edward's eulogy at the church service. She was asked to include something about Edward that wasn't necessarily positive – some habit or something she might have found annoying or irritating. She couldn't think of anything, and finally settled on the fact that he would empathize very strongly with everything, to the point where she'd find him sobbing in front of the television while watching the news and hearing of someone who had been hurt or killed.

During his last winter, the lock on the front door of Edward and Rosalie's condo building had broken somehow, and a homeless man started coming in to their foyer at night and sleeping there. Five of the six units were filled with people who were inclined to call the police and ask them to remove the man from the foyer.

It was no longer easy for Edward to communicate in writing, so he must have spent a fair amount of time writing a note for the man, telling him he understood that the man needed a warm place to sleep but explaining that it was not safe for the man or the condo residents to have him sleeping on the foyer floor. He told the man about a shelter, and included instructions about how he could get there, which involved a bus trip.

Realizing that the man would likely not have the money to take a bus, he taped a bus token to the note.

If I remember correctly, Rosalie found the note on Edward's bedside table after he died. I think the man was relocated before Edward finished or found time to drop the letter off in the foyer. I was with her, going through Edward's things not long after the funeral. I was mostly standing quietly, watching her meander through the surfaces, drawers and closets, hearing her occasional remarks (finding a partial package of the Depends that Edward had needed during his last days, she murmured, "There must be some needy incontinent people") and offering whatever help and support I could, which wasn't much.

I had to smile at the note, and I'm thinking Rosalie probably did too. It was a very Edward thing to do. I would have done the expedient thing, which would have involved the authorities, I'm sure, and I would have told myself that the man would be safely relocated more quickly and find a more reliable place to sleep in the bargain. Perhaps that would have been true, but Edward's solution was rooted in treating the man as he treated everyone – with respect, as an equal.

That note woke me up. The Chicago area has its share of homeless people. Before Edward, I gave those who asked what I could, and rushed on with my day. Since reading Edward's note, though, I never forget that they are deserving of the same courtesies and respect I afford to anyone else, whether I know them or not.

I've always thought I was a compassionate person, but I feel that Edward gave me something more that day. I hope so, because if that's the case, I'm carrying one of the best parts of him with me.

After they fall asleep I sit on the floor and cry

As much as I feel like I know Rosalie, I'm never 100% sure. I tend to take for granted that she is like me in certain ways and unlike me in others.

As I've said, we definitely have similar senses of humor. My brother told me a joke once. It goes like this:

"A man goes into a bar. As he's sitting at the bar, enjoying his drink, he notices a man at the end of the bar. The man is short, slight, has very black hair and a toothbrush mustache, and he seems to be speaking with a German accent. Finally the man watching him can't stand it anymore. He leaves his bar stool and walks over to the man, and says, "I apologize for bothering you, but I've been watching you, and I had to come over here and say – you look *exactly* like Adolf Hitler." The man replies, 'As a matter of fact, I am Adolf Hitler, and as soon as I finish my drink, I'm going to kill 6 million Jews and 4 acrobats.'"

At this point in the telling of the joke, Howard stopped. After a few seconds, I said something like, "And…" Howard asked if anything seemed strange in what he'd said, and I said I didn't get the part about the acrobats, to which he replied, "**See! Nobody cares about the Jews!**"

(As a Jewish person, I'm allowed to tell jokes like this. Don't try it at home…)

Anyway, I told this joke to Edward and Rosalie. Rosalie laughed long and loud, just as I had. Edward didn't find it even a little bit funny. I admit it's not going to appeal to everyone. But my point is that I knew Rosalie would appreciate it exactly as I had.

We both have a temper, and I think we've both learned how to control it, for the most part. I've seldom seen Rosalie angry, and even when she has been angry, she has been in control. There was some confusion at Edward's funeral and some of her relatives were kind of complaining about the way things were going, and she did raise her voice to one of her uncles. I found her a few minutes later in the ladies room, where she was already pretty much calmed down. Had I been in her situation and someone gave me a hard time about anything, I would have been off the rails until someone gave me a Valium.

I cry easily and often. When something bad happens to me or mine, I deal with it, but I do so with tears in my eyes, and frequently with tears streaming down my cheeks. Sometimes I cry first and take action later, sometimes it's simultaneous. But there is no pain, no sorrow, no anger in my existence that is not accompanied by tears, and here is where I always thought that Rosalie and I were different. I've almost never seen her cry. It's hard for me to imagine her crying.

Had I known her when we were teenagers, I would have been jealous of her apparent ever-present self-possession, but by now I've learned that my crying is a physical thing that I really have little or no control over, not a personality deficit. (And it makes my eyes look really green, but that's completely beside the point.)

The point, clearly, is that Rosalie is not a crier. I knew that things would have to be difficult for her with Edward gone. In the first weeks or months after the funeral, I really tried to spend time with her several nights a week. But at some point I always left and went back to my apartment to work or sleep, leaving her alone with two very young children. I took it for granted that she would be okay, that she would manage as she had always seemed to manage everything.

So imagine my complete surprise when, during a phone conversation about how she was coping, she was talking about Hayley and Claire and she said "Every night, after they fall asleep, I sit on the floor and cry."

I felt like someone had punched me in the stomach, causing me to lose my breath.

During all the time I spent with them throughout Edward's illness, I had, I think, subconsciously looked toward a day that Edward would be gone and I would go on with my life, concentrating on my business. I was doing that. I was actually working 7 days a week, trying to dig out from having underpaid my taxes during the first full year that I was self-employed. Having chosen to start a business with absolutely no idea about what I was doing, I found myself really enjoying working for myself and wanting to continue it for as long as possible.

Something had to give, and as it turned out, quite a lot gave. I spent less time with my mother and other members of my family, worked a minimum of 90 hours every week, slept almost not at all, and really just obsessed about work.

I believed that Rosalie would be fine. I would not have thrown myself so thoroughly into my work and what turned into a path toward a life partner for me if I had known that she needed me. By the time I realized, it was too late for me to go back. I had to do the work. Rosalie turned to another friend, Carol, who became a pivotal person for her, and for Hayley and Claire. I've often felt over the years that Carol usurped what should have been my position in their lives – but I know it happened because I allowed it to happen. At the time, I didn't see that I had a choice, and maybe making a different choice would have cost me my business. I'll never know. I just try to focus on the fact that Rosalie and I are still friends, I still feel that Hayley and Claire are as much part of me as they would have been had I given birth to them, and I hope that Rosalie is not harboring anger or resentment about the choices I've made, as much as she might be entitled to those feelings.

.

I've met someone

I lived alone from the time I left my mother's house in 1977 until 1999, when Larry moved from Logansport, Indiana to Chicago to live and work with me. (In case you're curious about where Logansport is, it's roughly 75 miles from anyplace fun in Indiana.)

During all the time that Edward and I were friends, I desperately wanted to have a loving, committed relationship with a man, and I never dated.

I didn't even think about dating during the years that Edward was ill, and when I started to think about it again after he had been gone a while, it had been so long since I had tried to interact with a man as anything other than a friend that I didn't know where to begin. Since I spent so much time using my computer, I decided to begin online, where I could be myself, I thought, and be judged by who I was, not how I looked.

I had been using AOL for a while, since it was the easiest way to get connected in those days, but I had avoided the chat rooms – I used my computer for business, and while I did start shopping online, I had never considered using it for social purposes. What changed my mind? Fear. I was afraid to meet men face to face. I was extremely heavy at the time, and I had not dated for well over seven years.

I made a few tentative forays into chat rooms which stopped very quickly because I was being stalked online by a guy who sent me very weird emails and threatening messages online. I had to create a new online identity for myself and move on.

I started experimenting with AOL dating message boards, which were a complete waste of time, except that I found an entire community of men who claimed to adore "big beautiful women." Most of the men I communicated with in the "BBW" chat rooms seemed… I think "weird" would be the technical term. I have a lifetime of mixed feelings about my body and my weight, but I don't want to be loved for my fat alone.

Moving on, I found an online dating service, Match.com. At that time, it was free, so I figured I had nothing to lose, even if I didn't hear from anyone. I created a profile and started contacting men and being contacted by them.

I met a number of men that way. A couple of them I liked well enough, a number of them I didn't like at all (Like the guy who was a chauffeur and owned two limos – he eventually set fire to one of his own cars because he had hired an African-American driver who he wanted to terminate. On the plus side, though, I always knew what the weather was like at the airport.), but either way it was fun for me to interact with men again. I had never particularly enjoyed it when I was younger, but now I had a stronger sense of myself and felt less urgent about the need to be with someone just so I didn't have to be alone. I had been alone for a long time and learned that I was okay that way.

When I signed on with Match.com, I was still very heavy. Fate stepped in via a gall bladder attack in 1996, during a period when I did not have health insurance. The doctor said I needed to have the gall bladder removed, but since I was diagnosed a few days before my insurance policy took effect, it was a pre-existing condition and I had to wait a year to have the surgery. The only way to avoid another attack, I was told, was to completely eliminate fat from my diet. Since the attack had been very painful and extremely scary, I was anxious to avoid another one, so the fat had to go.

Eliminating fat from your diet is not as easy as it might sound. Strawberries and bananas have fat. All meat, fish and poultry have fat. Pasta, unless it's made with rice flour, has fat. For the first few days I ate steamed vegetables and nothing else. Then I added baked potatoes and white rice. It's not a very healthy diet, but I had no choice.

It's virtually impossible to be on a fat-free diet and not lose weight. I lost 170 pounds in the 14 months between the attack and the surgery, so I was close to a normal size when I met some of those Match.com men, and my weight did not get in the way of getting to know them.

Rosalie got me through that year. She made the fat free diet palatable for me, finding a variety of foods and sauces I'd never heard of that added variety and flavor to an otherwise bland diet. More importantly, she supported me during the whole weight loss thing. It was ironic that, after a lifetime of struggling with my weight, I had reached a point in my life where I had decided not to ever try to lose weight again. I learned that I needed to accept my body as it was and eat when I was hungry and not for emotional reasons. Then I eliminated fat from my diet and started losing weight in spite of myself. It was quite surreal, and there were very few people I could talk to about it. Naturally, most people assumed that I'd be thrilled to be looking better.

The fact that I started dating meant that I spent less time with Rosalie and the girls, and I think that was hard for her. I know it was hard for me. She was getting closer to wanting to date again, too, and didn't have an opportunity to meet men, even if she had the time to get away from the girls and the money to hire babysitters. I felt bad that I was out having a good time and she was not.

At some point, she talked to me about the fact that she was feeling neglected by me, that I was making dates with strangers the next priority after my work and that left no time for her. I wasn't exactly meeting Mr. Right anyway and I didn't want her to feel abandoned by me, so I cut back for a while – until early September, when I called and told her, "I've met someone."

It's been nice knowing you

In September, I got a Match.com email from a guy named Larry. In it, he described himself as an educated man looking for the same in a woman. I read his description of himself on the Match.com site, which didn't say much, and wrote him back thanking him for his interest but telling him that while I consider myself intelligent, I did not have a college degree and therefore I might not be what he was looking for. He wrote back, saying, "Degree, schmegree – I just don't want to be with someone who has to ask for the number to dial 911."

After a semi-awkward first meeting date (a play and dinner afterward), we made plans to meet near the Indiana Dunes on a Sunday afternoon. The entire way there I was cursing myself and the traffic ("screaming myself hoarse in the car" might be a more apt description), thinking how much I hated driving to Indiana, how stupid it was to be fighting this kind of traffic for a total stranger, how I could be home working, etc. By the time I finally got to the mall where we were set to meet at an Applebee's for lunch, I was furiously sorry I'd agreed to come at all. Then I saw Larry in the parking lot and I felt better. It was a wonderful day, and suddenly, my life was different.

Things moved along pretty quickly from there. For the next year and a half we visited one another on weekends. Larry had serious job burnout and was fed up with Logansport, and he started looking for a job closer to Chicago. Unfortunately, there were not many jobs available in his field in his salary range, as he was very near the top of his field after 20 years in economic development. He looked into jobs that were farther away, and actually considered a position near Indianapolis, which is an additional 75 miles farther from Chicago than is

Logansport. He didn't tell me about it till there was an offer on the table, and while I left it up to him, I did say I didn't see our relationship continuing as it was with the additional distance between us.

By the time the offer near Indy came up, I wanted us to get married. This was kind of a surprise to me, because after living alone for over 20 years, I didn't know how to live with anyone, and I had only seen one good marriage up close. But I loved Larry and wanted to live with him, and we had agreed long before that neither of us wanted to live with someone without being married. For me, it wasn't a moral issue – I just felt that if I was going to make that kind of commitment, I'd go all the way or not at all.

After he decided to turn down the new job, we began talking more seriously about him coming to work with me. My consulting business was growing and I wanted someone with real business experience to help me grow the business more effectively. He was very resistant, probably for a lot of reasons. For him, it meant relocating, giving up a career he'd spent 20 years building, and moving forward with a relationship that was just 2 ½ years old. The whole prospect scared the hell out of me, and I was staying in the same area I'd lived all my life, and keeping my business.

Finally he took the plunge and quit his job. He moved into my Chicago apartment with me, but I started looking for a new place the day he gave notice. I found one in Schaumburg and rented it for a year. While this may not be the worst decision in the history of mankind, it is without question, as Larry would say, "in the team photo."

Rosalie was NOT happy about it. She had been a rock through my entire relationship with Larry, and maintained throughout that she was thrilled to see me happy. She was never anything but happy for me – until I told her I was moving to Schaumburg (25 miles away), to which she replied, "Well, Cheryl, it's been nice knowing you." I think she must have been angry and hurt, and I was scared out of my wits – I didn't want to live in Schaumburg and I had my doubts about everything I was doing – I would have much preferred to stay close to her, if I could have found an apartment large enough that we could afford, in which Larry could be happy.

I saw leaving the city as something I had to do for Larry. That was probably not true, but he was not enamored of my city apartment or the parking situation in my neighborhood. And it probably didn't help that, during a weekend that he was in town, some maniac drove through the area, shooting at people outside a temple few blocks away – those white supremacists can really ruin a Friday night.

So we moved. Man, I *hated* that place.... I liked the pond that our bedroom and dining room overlooked, but I hated Schaumburg, and the commute to get anywhere we needed to go was horrendous. I felt far away from my life and my friends, especially Rosalie. I needed Rosalie. I did indeed have problems adjusting to living with someone. I had assumed that living with someone meant that there were boundaries that had to be respected, and there were. But I didn't always know where the lines were drawn.

We only lived in Schaumburg for a year before buying our house which is only about 5 miles from Rosalie's condo. In November of 1999, a month after we moved in, Larry and I decided that we would get married in the Spring of 2000. Rosalie agreed to stand up with me and to allow Hayley and Claire to be flower girls, and I looked forward to a few months of love and laughter and wedding plans.

    It didn't all turn out quite the way I'd planned.

I want to be married in a house of God

May 5, 2000 was a wonderful day, in every way. At the end of the day, I felt like everything I went through to have the wedding I wanted had been worth it. And it was, completely, the way I wanted it.

I had expected my mother to be 100% happy for me, right from the beginning, and to share the entire experience with me. She had already played the mother of the bride role twice, once for Anne, a girl who worked with her, and once for my stepsister, Karen. I admit to having felt enormously jealous on both of those occasions, that my mother was being the mother of the bride for someone else. But I really thought if my turn ever came, she'd be more excited and involved than she ever could have been with Anne or Karen.

Instead, the day after I told her we had set a date, everything kind of fell to pieces. I told her that we were going to be married in a chapel at Fourth Presbyterian Church, and she got upset, but she wouldn't tell me why. She insisted that she wasn't bothered by me marrying a man who isn't Jewish, that she didn't care if I got married by a pastor or where I got married, as long as it wasn't anywhere in the church building.

I never considered changing my mind. I felt like this was the one time in my life where I was supposed to do what I wanted to do, and other people's feelings didn't factor in. I wanted very badly to get married in that chapel. The positive thing about the whole situation with my mother is that I was able to explore why it felt so important to me, because I wanted to make her understand, even if she didn't change her mind. I opted to do a lot of communicating via email, and this is what I told her:

Dear Mom,

I thought maybe I should let you know why I want to get married in the church, not so that you'll change what you feel -- I know that's got to come from within you or not at all -- but just so that you'll understand the thoughts and feelings that went into the decision.

As I think I told you, I got this idea last spring, or whenever I first visited the church as a prospective client. They were talking to me about the fact that they have joint services of some kind on the Jewish high holidays. It occurred to me as I was listening that if Larry and I got married at some point, our wedding should be like that -- a marrying of our religious backgrounds and feelings of spirituality as well as everything else that marriage entails. At that time, I did not think about actually getting married there -- just that if we did get married, having a Presbyterian pastor and a rabbi would be the best way to symbolize that part of our union.

I've been working closely with Fourth Church, and from the beginning, I've felt close to Sarah Sarchet, the associate pastor who I decided I wanted to ask to officiate at my wedding. Unlike most clients, from the beginning the people there have treated me like one of them. And because of who they are, they treat each other like family. So they took me in. I've gotten a sense of belonging at Fourth Church since the first time I went there. I feel comfortable within those walls.

When marriage starting seeming like something that would really happen for me, I knew right away that I wanted Sarah Jo to marry us, with a rabbi there with whom she's performed services, because I trust her enough to believe that if she feels good about him, I will too. So I started thinking about where I wanted the ceremony to be held and who I wanted to be there.

    The guest list was easy, and you were the first name on it and have been the first name on it in every fantasy or thought I've had about this in the past two years. When I started thinking about where, my first thoughts were an office of some kind, and I actually had a similar reaction to those thoughts as yours to the thought of my marrying in a church. I had to explore those feelings, and I realized two things: I need to feel at home wherever I do this, because this is a huge deal to me, and I really want to marry in a house of God.

I found that I was very uncomfortable with the impersonal sense of someone's office. So I rejected that idea. I moved on to a place like the Marriott and found that I still didn't feel right about it. Then, one day I was looking at those pictures of Grandpa and Edward that are now on my mantel during a time that I was thinking about us getting married. I was packing them, as a matter of fact, as Larry and I were preparing to move here, which I viewed as a step toward us getting married.

Grandpa's picture was the first thing I packed, and I was thinking as I was wrapping up the picture, about how important it is to me to still feel his presence in my life, and Edward's and Nathan's - that they were the first thing I thought about taking with me to my new life.

I believe that they are with God -- in His house -- and that I'll see them again someday. There have been times that I've held on very tightly to that belief, because it hurts me too much to think that they're just gone. I can't accept that. So I see them as being in God's house. And I believe that if I'm married in a house of God, they will all be with me in what feels like a very real way, and that will complete my guest list, because I couldn't get married without them there with me.

And I was right – Edward was with me that day. Not just in Hayley and Claire, though he will always be part of them; not just in the toast I gave, but with me. Right beside me. And I know how happy he was for me. I wish I could have seen him.

Crossing boundaries

One day, shortly after we returned from our honeymoon, I crossed a boundary I didn't know existed, and Larry talked about leaving me. I'm not sure whether I ever let myself get to the point where I believed this would never happen – I had been close to trusting him that much, but I guess I never really got there, because I wasn't as taken aback, or devastated, by the threat as I would have expected. I realized that some part of me must have been assuming all along that he would leave me.

Years of failed relationships, from my father on down, taught me that I was never important enough to anyone to stick with. I know in my head that this is a twisted and false view of reality, but for most of my life I have had a deep-seated fear of being left. Not even so much just being left, but the idea that one wrong move on my part could result in my being left. I still have this fear. I've accepted the fact that I always will.

That's why, I know, I was so hurt when I told Rosalie that I was moving with Larry to the suburbs, 25 miles away, and her response was "Well, Cheryl, it's been nice knowing you."

Rosalie must have felt (and may still, I guess) some of the same abandonment issues that I do, and she has more right to them. Edward did leave her, after all, with 2 children who weren't even two years old. Her mother left her with her father and brother after a divorce, her father moved from his apartment on the second floor of the building she lived in at a time when it was clear that Rosalie needed him badly....

My list is shorter – my father left our family when I was 18, and every boy/man I tried to get close to from then on left me. Nothing Freudian about that, right? All those relationships were short and unsatisfying, so while I felt abandoned, I didn't particularly miss the men themselves.

On the other hand, I have to say that I really missed living around the corner from Rosalie. If one of us needed the other, we were right there.

Now, even though my life is so different, I miss it more than before, probably. When Larry threatened to leave, I wanted to see Rosalie. Not because she could do anything or would necessarily have any words of advice, and not because I really needed any advice – just because she loves me and she would care. It wouldn't matter that I'd get over it, that I knew Larry didn't really want to leave. She's my friend, she loves me, and she'd care.

This all happened a few weeks after we returned from our honeymoon. I was waiting for our wedding pictures to arrive, and in the midst of my horror over the threatened abandonment, I was struck by the thought that only I could fail so miserably that my marriage would be over before the pictures came back.

I survived and forgave Larry silently for what that conversation did to me. And our wedding pictures came back, finally. While I of course was not particularly happy with the way I looked in them, they are beautiful pictures. I had occasion to look through them numerous times, to select pictures to reprint for various people, and I caught myself more than once – I was looking for Edward.

Because he died

Since I was very young, people have told me that when I set my mind to do something, I will not stop until I have succeeded in doing what I set out to do. This is pretty much true. I'm stubborn, and I'm close to a complete failure at... failure.

My early twenties were a difficult time for me. My father had remarried and I felt excluded from his life. My mother was dating (and later married) a man that I hated. I had a job that I hated so much that I cried on my way to work and again on my way home. Every day.

I started seeing a counselor shortly after my 25th birthday. My mother called me to say she wanted me to give her a present for my birthday (as she had given birth to me so I could have birthdays) and go and see someone who might be able to make me feel better.

I went to Jewish Community Services, who had a sliding pay scale based on your income, and was "assigned" to Katherine Bloomfield, who looked like she was about my age.

When I started, I told her my goals for counseling were to get thin and get married. As it turned out, there were many things to deal with before either of those issues was addressed. Both of us went through a lot of changes in those years, although most of mine were internal. I went through being fired, a short period of unemployment, 3 job changes, 3 moves, several weight losses and gains, the deaths of my grandfather, my nephew and Edward, and a marriage. Katherine went through a couple of office moves, a marriage and the births of 3 children. I'm sure she went through many other things, too, but she knew a lot more about me than I did about her.

So I was seeing Katherine when Edward was

diagnosed, throughout his illness and after his death. From the time that Rosalie called and told me that Edward was gone, I focused on what I could do for her and with her to help her keep it together and get through the next days and months. I don't think I let myself think very much about Edward or feel my own sense of loss – I didn't feel entitled to it, somehow.

After some time had passed I did start to feel my loss more and more. On some level, I was aware of feeling angry. I talked to Katherine about it, and suddenly found myself crying uncontrollably and ranting angrily about how useless I had been, saying "I did everything I could think of to do. I helped them as much as I could, I spent as much time with them as I could, and none of it was enough. I didn't do enough, it was all for nothing."

Katherine asked me why I felt like I hadn't done enough, why it was all for nothing.

"Because he died," I said.

As soon as I heard myself speak the words, I knew how wrong they were, but I felt them to be real. Some part of me really believed that if I tried hard enough and wanted it enough, Edward would not die. Once I set my mind to something, I don't give up until I succeed.

It's dangerous to believe your own press clippings. I thought, throughout Edward's illness, that I was being pragmatic, accepting the fact that he would die too young, that I would lose one of the most important people in my life.

I know in my head that Edward's death was not my failure and that I never had any control over his illness or its outcome. But I think there's still a place in my heart that isn't so sure.

Halcyon days

I read a lot as a kid. I still do, but not nearly as much as I did before adulthood derailed so much of my free time. When I was around eight, while my friends were heavily into the Beezuz and Ramona books and their ilk, I was frequently to be found reading books about teenage girls.

I was crushingly shy as a child. I was afraid of nearly everyone, particularly other children my age. I remember once passing a school playground while in the back seat of a car my dad was driving. He pointed to the children playing and running around having fun at recess and asked if I would like to go there. I burst into years.

My parents claim that I taught myself to read when I was three. If this is true, I'm sure it was a defense mechanism, since if I had my nose in a book all the time, I didn't have to look at people and know they were looking at me.

In any case, I looked forward to being a teenager. I read books about teenagers who had been shy and outgrown it, so I was always looking for further evidence that my complete lack of social skills was not a birth defect. Also, it seemed like these teenagers had the times of their lives. They went to the beach, had picnics, ate at malt shops, wore makeup, dated cute boys… Who wouldn't want to be them?

One of the books I read featured a very smart boy who, of course, the book's heroine had a star-crossed relationship with before they finally ended up together at the end. The boy took the girl to the beach and as they were sitting side by side watching the gulls fly overhead, he said "Halcyon days." Cass, the heroine, asked what he meant, and he explained.

Halcyon is a name for a bird of Greek legend which is commonly associated with the kingfisher. The phrase comes from the ancient belief that fourteen days of calm weather were to be expected around the winter solstice - usually 21st or 22nd of December in the Northern Hemisphere. as that was when the halcyon calmed the surface of the sea in order to brood her eggs on a floating nest.

Halcyon means calm and tranquil, or 'happy or carefree'. It is rarely used now apart from in the expression halcyon days. The name of the legendary bird was actually alcyon, the 'h' was added in regard to the supposed association with the sea ('hals' in Greek).

Definition courtesy of www.phrases.org.uk

I read that book so many times that the pages started to fall out. I **yearned** for a halcyon day. I don't remember ever feeling carefree as a child, so I pinned my hopes on becoming a teenager.

Things didn't go so swimmingly in my teenage years either, so I can't say I had any halcyon days before I finished my formal education. But I never forgot the concept, and in adulthood, it became real in two ways.

Mary Chapin Carpenter, one of my favorite artists, included the phrase "halcyon days" in one of her songs. I would have loved that song anyway, but hearing the long-remembered phrase and attaching its meaning to my life as an adult was a wondrous experience for me.

I played the song over and over after Edward died. It implies someone speaking about how things will be near the end of their life, and how they'll look back on the past as a better time – halcyon days.

Edward made at least one of my girlhood yearnings a reality. Every day I spent with him was a halcyon day.

Afterword

When someone is frail, most people's instinct is to step back. Real friends come closer. You have been the best of the best.

The words were spoken by my friend Edward in a whisper. I had to lean over the railing of his rented hospital bed to hear them. We were in the living room of a third floor condo, it was a stiflingly hot August day in Chicago, and there was no air conditioning. I didn't notice.

When I saw him the next day he could no longer speak, and the day after that he was in a coma.

And then he died.

After Edward became ill, there was not a minute that I spent with him and Rosalie for any reason other than that I wanted to be there. I wanted to help, I wanted to be able to make a difference, make things easier. I wanted him to live. I wanted to give him, and Rosalie and Hayley and Claire, some relief, pleasure, peace of mind – whatever I could. And I wanted to be with my friends, to capture whatever memories I could in the time I had.

I should have known that ultimately, I would be getting more than I was able to give. In 23 words, Edward found a way to say everything – Thank you, I forgive you, I love you, I'll miss you, I'll remember you, you are my friend.

Wherever you are, you will always be with me

Made in the USA
Charleston, SC
12 July 2010